**NATIONAL GEOGRAPHIC**

# School Today and Long Ago

Mario Lucca

My great great grandpa lived a long time ago.
When he went to school,
he carried his book in his hand.

2

I carry my books in my bag.

3

When my great great grandpa went to school…

...his classroom looked like this.

This is my classroom.

When my great great grandpa went to school, he sat at a wooden desk.

9

I sit on a chair at my desk.

When my great great grandpa went to school,
he wrote with chalk.
He wrote on a slate.

I write with a pencil.
I write on paper.

11

When my great great grandpa went to school, he liked his teacher.

I like my teacher, too.